An Anti-State Christmas

Tom Mullen

For everyone whose lack of faith the state finds

disturbing.

CONTENTS

1   A GREAT LIBERTARIAN IS BORN   1

2   JESUS DUNKS ON THE RIGHT   8

3   JESUS DUNKS ON THE LEFT   20

4   LIBERTARIAN CHRISTMAS SPECIALS   29

5   THE REAL HERO OF 'IT'S A WONDERFUL   37
    LIFE'

6   DICKENS' A CHRISTMAS CAROL: TOO SAD   48
    AN ENDING FOR THE SEASON

7   AN ANTI-STATE CHRISTMAS   57

    ABOUT THE AUTHOR   85

Tom Mullen

CHAPTER 1

A GREAT LIBERTARIAN IS BORN

It's not a surprise that **libertarian themes pervade many iconic Christmas specials.** After all, they celebrate the birthday of one of the great libertarians of all time.

In the Gospels, government is exposed as evil right from Jesus' birth. While Jesus is still an infant, a paranoid King Herod is willing to kill all of the babies in his kingdom to eliminate the perceived threat to his power represented by Jesus.

Tax collectors are de facto sinners in the gospels, on a par with prostitutes. Libertarians would consider this unfair to prostitutes, but for the times this couldn't land better.

Jesus himself doesn't disappoint, either. From the moment he begins his ministry, he wages a nonstop verbal war against the hypocritical, oppressive, tax-devouring Temple priests. Jews at the time were required to pay annual taxes to the priests and were also expected to come and make sacrifices at the Jerusalem Temple. To do so, they had to buy the livestock for the sacrifices from the priests and deal with the priests' money changers.

That's why the libertarian from Galilee kicked the money changers out. This would have been considered a revolutionary act.

One can't help but equate Jerusalem at that time with Washington, DC today: an entire city of tax-fed, opulent wealth.

Jesus has no patience for excessive regulation, either. When he encounters a Jewish law that does not address actual criminal activity, he encourages his followers to break it. When the meddling scribes confront Jesus with allowing his disciples to eat without washing their hands, Jesus lets loose with his customary anti-government invective, calling them hypocrites and then instructing "the people" to ignore this idiotic law and focus on not committing real crimes instead. (Mark 7:1-23)

Jesus doesn't have much use for social conservatives. When they bring a woman who has committed adultery before him to be stoned, he shames them into letting her go (John 8:1-7). He does not condone her sin, nor imply that she may not be judged by God for it. He makes a distinction between those actions which constitute harm to other human beings and can therefore be punished by men and those which do not constitute harm and can only be judged by God.

Jesus shows no such objection to the law against theft, committed by the men crucified with him. Unlike adultery, this constitutes harm against the property of others. One of the thieves says that he is justifiably punished, and Jesus does not contradict him. He offers forgiveness but not escape from punishment (Luke 23:40-43).

Michael Moore seems to think that Jesus' message is inconsistent with free enterprise. Perhaps Mr. Moore should read the gospels again. The heroes in most of Jesus' parables are businessmen and property owners. The villains, like the evil vinedressers in Mark 12:1-12, are those looking for unearned wealth. The beauty of this story is that it affirms property ownership on the literal level and simultaneously represents a symbolic shot at the corrupt Temple priests.

The third steward of Matthew 25:14-30 is punished for *not* being a capitalist. Again, there is a symbolic meaning here, but Jesus chooses a free enterprise-friendly vehicle to convey his message.

While Jesus says that wealth can be a distraction, he unambiguously states that it is not a sin in and of itself. Jesus has many wealthy friends, including the wealthy women who support him and his disciples during his ministry (Luke 8:3). He does not consider them sinners as he does those who derive their wealth from taxation. If only today's "liberals" would learn this distinction.

While Jesus often encourages people to *voluntarily* give to the poor, he never once implies that this should be accomplished by forced redistribution – certainly not through the Jewish government he spends the rest of the gospels criticizing.

Even during his passion, Jesus continues to make libertarians stand up and cheer. Anticipating the 5th Amendment by over 1700 years, Jesus refuses to talk to the cops or give evidence against himself. In John 18:20 he basically says, "If you have some proof, present it. You're not getting anything from me." He likewise refuses to talk to Pontius Pilate.

The result? Acquittal. Pilate "finds no case against this man." Of course, both the Roman and the Jewish governments break their own laws and Jesus gets crucified anyway, providing another libertarian lesson about the reliability of most governments to follow their own rules.

Whether they believe in God or not, all libertarians have good reason to celebrate the birth of Jesus Christ. If only more Americans would be Christ-like by holding the government in contempt, resisting its ridiculous edicts, rebelling against its wealth redistribution, and honoring free enterprise, we'd all be a lot freer here in the "land of the free."

And if we observed the one rule this great libertarian gave us on dealing with one another, "Do unto others as you would have them do unto you," we'd live in a safer, more peaceful world.

Merry Christmas to all.

CHAPTER 2

JESUS DUNKS ON THE RIGHT

"Then the scribes and the Pharisees brought a woman who had been caught in adultery and made her stand in the middle. They said to him, "Teacher, this woman was caught in the very act of committing adultery. Now in the law, Moses commanded us to stone such women. So what do you say?" They said this to test

him, so that they could have some charge to bring against him. Jesus bent down and began to write on the ground with his finger. But when they continued asking him, he straightened up and said to them, "Let the one among you who is without sin be the first to throw a stone at her." Again he bent down and wrote on the ground. And in response, they went away one by one, beginning with the elders. So he was left alone with the woman before him. Then Jesus straightened up and said to her, "Woman, where are they? Has no one condemned you?" She replied, "No one, sir." Then Jesus said, "Neither do I condemn you. Go, (and) from now on do not sin anymore." (John 8: 3-11)

As we approach the new year with conservatism again ascendant in the political sphere, this story of Jesus' uncompromising libertarianism seems even more timely than stories of his birth, despite the approach of his celebrated birthday.

Nowhere does Jesus admonish "social conservatives" more harshly.

There is an important distinction here. By "social conservative," I do not mean anyone who disapproves of certain human behavior. The freedom to follow the dictates of one's conscience was the first inalienable right recognized by the founders of our republic. If one truly believes that homosexuality, adultery, or other "non-conservative" behavior violates the laws of God, it is that person's inalienable right to disapprove of it, even to voice his disapproval of it, regardless of the anguished cries of the social justice thought police.

However, no one has a right to use violence against those who engage in behavior that does not violate the property rights of another person, regardless of whether or not that behavior violates the laws of God. Since all laws are enforced under the threat of violence (as this story illustrates wonderfully), Jesus makes clear in this passage that it is not for men to enforce the laws of God. With the exception of cases in which one human being has done injury to another, the right to punish human behavior is reserved for God. Insofar as the adultery involved violating a marriage contract, there may be a civil dispute to be settled, but certainly not criminal punishment.

It is important to recognize that Jesus does not condone the sin the anonymous woman committed. When he has shamed away the mob who would have stoned her, Jesus commands her to sin no more. Neither does he insinuate that her behavior might not have consequences for her soul. With flawless libertarian reasoning, Jesus teaches us the true meaning of freedom: that God grants us the liberty to do as we wish, even to reject him and his laws, but that we also bear the full consequences of our actions. If we harm another person, then we are subject to the laws of men. However, it is otherwise left to each individual to determine the will of God according to his conscience and to choose whether to act accordingly or not. There never has been nor can there ever be any body of corruptible men who can save an individual's soul.

This is by no means the only place in the gospels that Jesus teaches us this lesson. His entire public ministry was one condemnation after another of the hypocritical, socially conservative theocracy. Indeed, it is the Jewish state that is Jesus' chief antagonist throughout the gospels. He is noticeably disinterested in the more secular Roman government, despite its tyranny over his people. While he certainly doesn't approve of the Romans, he has no interest in political revolution. As Jesus tells Pilate, "my kingdom is not of this world." (John 18:36). However, his own government does not merely commit secular, political oppression against its people. It usurps the authority of God and attempts to judge in his place. For this, Jesus constantly lets loose his most venomous reproaches.

Throughout the gospels, "the chief priests and Pharisees" are constantly shown up for what they are. They do not seek to punish sins to defend the honor of God, but for their own selfish political motives. Their persecution and eventual murder of Jesus himself is quite obviously perpetrated out of fear of his influence over the people. And what is this subversive influence that warrants torture and death? "Love one another as I have loved you. Love your enemies. Do unto others as you would have them do unto you." Of course, the state would hate such a message. It runs afoul of every depravity to which the state tries to exhort its citizens, including its wars, its persecution of non-conformists, and its rampant looting of the citizenry dressed up as "public works."

When Jesus encounters man-made laws masquerading as the laws of God, he openly condones breaking those laws. When his disciples pick fruit on the Sabbath and are caught in the act by the Pharisees, Jesus beats the Pharisees at their own game by citing Jewish scripture, which describes David eating sacred bread out of the temple, reserved for the priests by Jewish law.

Demonstrating how perverse any theocratic state eventually becomes, the Pharisees then bring a man forward with a "withered hand," daring Jesus to cure him and break the law himself. They are willing to see this man miss his one chance to be cured so they can use their distorted interpretation of God's command to "keep holy the Sabbath" to ensnare Jesus for political ends. Jesus breaks the law without hesitation, saying that "it is lawful to do good on the Sabbath." Caring little for the wisdom of the lesson and interested only in maintaining their own autocratic power, the Pharisees withdraw to begin planning Jesus' murder. (Matthew 12: 1-14)

By attempting to use the law to enforce their morality, social conservatives violate the very principles they say they cherish most. Social conservatives decry Islam because it attempts to "propagate the faith by the sword." However, there is only a cosmetic difference between promoting your religious views through acts of terrorism and doing likewise with laws against victimless crimes enforced by the threat of "legal" violence by the state. In both cases, it is the sword that compels the victim rather than the mind or the heart. Neither can social conservatives rely on the argument that their laws are passed by an elected body representing the people. If that justifies socially conservative laws, then what is their objection to the welfare state?

No part of this argument should be misconstrued as an endorsement of political correctness or the left-wing agenda to grant positive rights to their own special interest groups. If we are truly a free society and believe in the first amendment to the U.S. Constitution, then every individual, whether the most fundamentalist Christian or the most libertine atheist, should have the right to speak freely, even if what they say offends another person. For many devout Christians, it is their sacred duty to try to persuade their fellow man to repent of his sins and embrace Jesus as his savior.

However, there is an ocean of difference between persuasion and coercion. The minute we say, "there ought to be a law," we are picking up the sword. If we do so in defense of legitimate property rights, we are within our rightful authority. If we do so to supplant the authority of God, we become the very type of people that Jesus spent his life fighting against. To truly be Christian, one must recognize the need for "a wall of separation between church and state."

Jesus was very clear about his views on what would lead to salvation and what would not. Jesus condemned many behaviors, like adultery, that social conservatives likewise condemn. He also said that "no one comes to the Father except through me." (John 14:6) However, he does not go on to say, "Therefore, if your brother does not come to me willingly, then draw your sword and force him." Salvation must be chosen; God did not create a race of slaves.

As we celebrate the birth of this great libertarian, let us not forget the lesson of his life and death. Jesus was murdered by the theocratic state for exposing their hypocrisy and resisting their unjust, blasphemous laws. Let us follow his example of speaking our minds according to our consciences but never resorting to force to save our brothers' souls. Each one of us will ultimately find that our understanding of the will of God is imperfect, as we are imperfect. Therefore, we must follow Jesus' example of tolerance and forgiveness, lest we find that we ourselves have mistakenly punished the innocent. Our laws should keep us from harming each other and leave each person's soul to the judgment of God.

CHAPTER 3

JESUS DUNKS ON THE LEFT

Socialists have long claimed Jesus as one of their own, arguing capitalism is antithetical to his message of universal brotherhood and care for the poor. One of the more authoritative examples was Pope Francis' 2013 EVANGELII GAUDIUM, in which he is critical of free markets. Reactions by Christian proponents of capitalism ranged from respectful disagreement to full-on denial that he was critical of capitalism at all.

The latter group is not facing reality. While later stating he is not Marxist, the pope clearly rejected a laissez faire approach to markets in favor of the highly regulated, redistributionist model promoted by the left. His offering is chock full of the usual sophisms leftists use to justify overriding freedom of choice in exchanges of property.

There is no need to address each of the pope's arguments against free markets from a purely economic perspective. Plenty of free market advocates have already done so. Tom Woods did a particularly thorough job on an episode of his podcast, The Tom Woods Show.

What is more surprising than the pope's leftist economic ideas is his ability to ignore the overtly pro-capitalist themes in the gospels themselves. Jesus' teaching consistently holds capitalists up as heroes. He never once even hints that the government should direct economic affairs.

The misconception that Jesus' message is anti-capitalist likely stems from the same confusion that pervades all leftist thinking: the inability to distinguish voluntary from coerced human action. Jesus often exhorts his followers to *voluntarily* give to the poor. But nowhere in the gospels does he suggest that the Romans or the vassal Jewish government should be empowered to tax others to provide for them.

Tax collectors are de facto sinners, remember?

Jesus also warns against the temptations that accompany great wealth. Being consumed with accumulating wealth to the exclusion of all other concerns leaves no room for devotion to God or charity to one's fellow man. This is summed up in Luke 16:13 when Jesus says,

> "No one can serve two masters. Either you will hate the one and love the other, or you will be devoted to the one and despise the other. You cannot serve both God and money."

Again, Jesus charges his followers to *manage their own* passion for wealth. There is no suggestion the government should be involved.

Jesus doesn't expound on political economy because, as he told Pilate, "my kingdom is not of this world." (John 18:36). However, his parables have consistently pro-capitalist themes.

In the parable of the bags of gold (Matthew 25: 14-30), the servants who choose to be capitalists with the master's money are richly rewarded upon the master's return. The servant who chose not to be a capitalist is not only not rewarded, he is "cast into the outer darkness, where there will be weeping and gnashing of teeth!"

Certainly, the story is symbolic. The money in the story represents the abilities given to each individual by God. But even on that level the story does not support the anti-capitalists. First, the master, the ultimate capitalist in the parable, actually represents God. Certainly, Jesus would have found another way to make his point if capitalists were de facto sinners (like tax collectors).

Notice also that the servant who chooses not to invest the master's money is the one given the least. Symbolically, he represents the person who has the least natural gifts or who is born to disadvantage. Does Jesus suggest that the other two servants should be taxed to help him? No. The most disadvantaged servant is expected to do the best with what he has. He isn't punished because he achieves less. He is punished because he fails to try.

In two other parables, Jesus represents God as the owner of a vineyard. In Matthew 20: 1-16, he makes the point that it is never too late for salvation and that a repentant man can claim it the same salvation as one who has been devout all of his life. He represents salvation as wages paid to laborers. When a laborer who worked longer complains that he is paid no more than one who only worked an hour, the master replies,

"Friend, I do thee no wrong: didst not thou

agree with me for a penny?

Take that thine is, and go thy way: I will give unto this last, even as unto thee."

Again, the message is spiritual, but Jesus conveys it via the very libertarian, capitalist idea that no one is entitled to any more wages than both parties *voluntarily* agree to.

God is again depicted as the owner of a vineyard in Matthew 21: 33-41. In this parable, the vineyard owner is even more overtly capitalist. Verse 33 in particular highlights that it is the previous work of the owner in planting the vineyard, hedging around it, and building a tower that makes the land productive before it is ever rented out to the husbandmen.

In other words, the capitalist had sacrificed his own consumption in the present to invest in land

and capital goods to improve the productivity of the land in the future. This has created an opportunity for the husbandmen to be more productive working on the owner's land than they would be on their own, without the land or the capital goods the owner has provided.

The owner then enters a voluntary agreement with the husbandmen whereby each party keeps part of what is produced. Both owner and husbandmen benefit from the agreement. The owner is entitled to the profits because he is the one who created the opportunity by sacrificing his own consumption in the past.

The husbandmen are evil specifically because they act like 20th century Marxists and renege on the agreement. They kill the owner's agents and even his son, hoping to seize *all* of the wealth for themselves.

In verse 41, Jesus teaches that the owner will destroy the Marxists and rent the land to other husbandmen *who will make him profits.* The right of the owner to profits is affirmed while the idea the workers are being exploited or are entitled to more than the owner has agreed to pay them is completely absent.

Nowhere in *any* of these parables are socialist ideas advanced. On the contrary, God is consistently represented as a capitalist and his children judged by how profitable they are to Him.

While the purpose of the parables is to teach a spiritual lesson, these are not the literary tools an anti-capitalist author would employ. Jesus' pro-capitalist bias couldn't hit one over the head any harder, which begs the question:

What Bible is Pope Francis reading?

CHAPTER 4

LIBERTARIAN CHRISTMAS SPECIALS

"And it came to pass that there went out a decree from Caesar Augustus that all the world should be taxed. And all went to be taxed, everyone to his own city, for to disobey the Roman emperor meant certain death."

The message in the opening lines of _The Little Drummer Boy_ (1968) is as rich and pleasing to the ear as Greer Garson's euphonious narration.

First, that Bethlehem was so crowded and there was "no room at the inn" for Joseph and Mary was not at all a natural occurrence. It was caused by the government, like virtually all human misery. Second, the passage reminds us that all taxation occurs under the threat of violence, for to refuse to pay would result in "certain death."

This is all within the first 30 seconds of the film. A libertarian couldn't ask for a better start.

Taxation is repeatedly denounced throughout the story. Garson continues by noting, "There were good people who could ill afford the cruel tax." Even the film's chief villain, Ben Haramad (voice by Jose Ferrer), who kidnaps Aaron in order to compel him to perform in his traveling show, addresses his audience as "fellow taxpayers," indicating that as bad as he might be, he is one with his audience in suffering under a much crueler and more malicious oppressor.

The Little Drummer boy is certainly edgy, as Jesus himself often was, and provides a very age-appropriate introduction to the gospel stories for young children. With the central lesson of Thanksgiving – that communism is lethal and private property essential to human survival – effectively erased from popular consciousness, it was refreshing to see these foundational libertarian ideas surviving in a classic Christmas special.

The same <u>DVD compilation</u> includes another classic, ***<u>Santa Claus is Comin' to Town</u>*** (1970). This one doesn't disappoint, either. Once again, the general misery within the aptly named "Sombertown" has the same source: government. One cannot help but see the parallels between Burgermeister Meisterburger's idiotic law against toys and the U.S. government's War on Drugs. All of the familiar characteristics are there.

First, the law is completely ineffective in stopping the children of Sombertown from playing with toys, aided by a young, energetic Kris Kringle. When the government confiscates the toys, Kringle brings more. When the government starts searching houses, Kringle hides the toys in stockings hanging by the fire.

Of course, each government failure to prevent people from engaging in activity that is harmless to others results in ever more oppressive measures. As they do today in the "land of the free," the government eventually resorts to "no knock raids," with armed men breaking down the doors of innocent and guilty alike. Parents and children huddle together in fear.

Meisterberger demonstrates government hypocrisy when he breaks his own law by playing with a yo-yo given to him by Kringle. What an effective analogy for the government's own involvement in drug trafficking, both by street cops "gone bad" and by the CIA in its vast covert operations. One also can't help thinking of the many federal and state officials caught disobeying their Covid-19 stay-at-home orders or mask mandates.

Meisterburger further emulates the U.S. government with ridiculous overreach in enforcing his unjust law, arresting not only Kris Kringle, but his whole family, his future wife Jessica and even the reformed Winter Warlock. All are charged with "conspiracy," a tactic routinely utilized by the government to circumvent the rules of evidence in court and put over 2 million people in prison.

The story also features a useful idiot in Jessica, who at first blindly supports the law, until Kringle gives her a porcelain doll. Realizing how harmless to others is her enjoyment of the doll, she finally begins to question the wisdom of prohibition.

Kringle escapes the dungeon with the help of the Winter Warlock's flying reindeer and remains an outlaw for many years afterwards. However, the story ends happily as the libertarians outlast the oppressive Meisterbergers, who eventually "died off and fell out of power." As narrator Fred Astaire relates,

"By and by, the good people realized how silly the Meisterberger laws were. Well, everybody had a wonderful laugh and then forgot all about them."

If only the good people of the United States would attain similar wisdom.

Within this pleasant little Christmas story, youngsters couldn't be taught a more radical libertarian lesson. The government is evil. Its edicts are often unjust and result in needless misery. The hero of the story is an outlaw who practices civil disobedience to bring a little happiness to his fellow man. Regardless of your feelings on drug prohibition, there are a thousand other parallels to real world government oppression.

Conservatives often complain that modern Christmas specials have scrubbed Jesus Christ out of the holiday, turning it into a secular celebration of gift giving and merrymaking. That's not hard to understand coming out of "progressive" modern Hollywood, whose animosity towards Christianity rivals its animosity towards free enterprise. It also explains why these wonderfully libertarian themes have disappeared from today's politically correct holiday fluff.

Whatever your religious beliefs, even if you have none at all, you can't go wrong watching these classic Christmas specials with your children. Not only will they learn the true meaning of Christmas, but they will be exposed at a young age to the founding American principle that government is evil.

God bless us, everyone.

CHAPTER 5

THE REAL HERO OF 'IT'S A WONDERFUL LIFE'

December is upon us and that means plentiful opportunities to watch the enduring classic, <u>It's a Wonderful Life</u>. Unfortunately, the overwhelming majority of viewers completely misinterpret Frank Capra's dystopian nightmare as a heartwarming Christmas tale.

The emotional appeal of angels getting their wings is undeniable. Crying out for correction, however, are the vicious slanders regarding the film's real hero, Henry Potter.

We first hear of Potter from George Bailey's father, Peter Bailey, who badmouths Potter with the usual falsehoods about businessmen. But during Bailey's envious rant, we learn something important: Henry Potter is a board member of the building and loan. We later learn Potter is, in fact, a stockholder.

That puts a somewhat different light on his subsequent motion to liquidate the business upon Peter Bailey's death. Yes, we hear George Bailey repeating the familiar socialist tropes his father did: that Potter only wants to close the building and loan because he "can't get his hands on it" and considers the little people cattle, etc. But Potter responds with some rather inconvenient facts: the building and loan has been making bad business decisions, providing what we'd now call subprime loans to people who can't pay them back.

We don't know how Potter became a stockholder, but the Bailey Building and Loan does not appear to be a publicly traded company. The most likely explanation is Peter Bailey asked Potter for capital, just as George Bailey does later in the film, in between rounds of disparaging Potter as a greedy capitalist. That would be perfectly consistent with "progressives" like the Bailey's today, who rail against capitalists out of one side of their face while sucking up to them for money out of the other.

But regardless of how Potter became a

stockholder, Peter Bailey has a fiduciary duty to him to run the business for maximum profit, providing Potter and the other stockholders a return on their investments, something George Bailey confirms they never intended to do. Instead, the Baileys squander their investors' money on a do-gooder, subprime loan scheme to make everyone a homeowner. It worked out in fictional Bedford Falls about as well as it did in early 2000s America.

Meanwhile, the Baileys constantly slander Potter's rental houses as "overpriced slums." These are the same Baileys whose housing opportunities are more expensive than Potter's.

Their accusations constantly beg the question: If Potter's houses are so bad, why do so many people choose to live in them? It's constantly implied

Potter's customers have no other choice, but what exactly does that mean? Why has no one else, including any of the businessmen on the board of the Bailey Building and Loan, developed rental properties that are higher in quality, lower in price, or both?

The inescapable truth is Potter is wealthy because he provides a product that most satisfies his customers' preferences for quality and price. If there were an opportunity to provide a higher quality product at a lower price than Potter was charging, a competitor would do so and take market share away from Potter, until Potter either raised his quality, lowered his price, or both.

The Baileys burn with resentment that so many residents of Bedford Falls prudently choose to live in Potter's less expensive housing than buy a house they can't afford, financed by the Baileys' Ponzi scheme. Thus, even after shirking their fiduciary duty to run the business properly, the Baileys spend decades assaulting Potters character in a transparent attempt to lure away his customers.

When the Depression hits and the Bailey Building and Loan is exposed for the fractional reserve fraud it is, Potter offers to come to the rescue with a generous offer to buy out its customers. It is noteworthy that there is a run on the Bailey Building and Loan and the local bank, but Potter is financially secure enough to save them both, proving once again he is the only honorable businessman in the film.

But we must give the devil his due. George Bailey, the ultimate huckster, saves the building and loan without Potter's help, convincing the yokel mob making a run on his business to keep their money tied up in his fundamentally insolvent confidence game.

That brings us to Potter's one regrettable act, which is concealing the $8,000.00 the incompetent Billy Bailey inadvertently handed him while attempting to make a deposit. It's true this was underhanded, although not unprovoked.

We don't know how much Potter had invested in the Building and Loan to become a stockholder, but suspect it was a lot more than $8,000. One could make the case he was merely getting back some of the money the Baileys had previously defrauded him of, but there are courts for such matters and Potter should have sought their help if he had a case.

Nevertheless, two generations of Baileys had

led a decades-long assault on Potter's good name, resulting in most townspeople disliking him, even though he has quite literally saved their lives on numerous occasions. Without him, a large portion of Bedford Falls would be unemployed or have nowhere to live. It is not an exaggeration to say that without Henry Potter, Bedford Falls would cease to exist. Yet, thanks to the Baileys, he is the most hated man in town.

Compare Potter's vindictive reaction when George Bailey crawls to him for help after the $8,000.00 is lost to Potter's reaction at the board meeting at the beginning of the movie. At the board meeting, Potter dismisses George's unhinged attack upon him and redirects the discussion to the subject of the meeting: what is best for Bedford Falls. By the latter confrontation, Potter tries to have George arrested for embezzling.

Potter's dastardly act is totally out of character with the Potter of the earlier scene or any other event we know of in Potter's life. As far as we know, he has always been a hard-nosed, unsentimental businessman, but has never committed a crime or held a grudge as he does now. Everything we know about Potter up to this point tells us his vindictive attempt to have George Bailey prosecuted is precisely the kind of emotional decision-making Potter has avoided for most of his life, which is why he is so wealthy at the beginning of the film.

Everyone has a breaking point. Potter had evidently reached his. Had he been prosecuted for keeping the $8,000.00 - tricky from a legal standpoint, since Billy Bailey literally handed him the money - he could easily have plead temporary insanity caused by years of psychological warfare waged against him by the Baileys.

We'll never know, because before Potter has any opportunity to allow his passion to cool and to clear up the misunderstanding, George Bailey sets off on his suicide melodrama, followed by a long, self-aggrandizing hallucination about angels and how Bedford Falls would be worse without him. By the time he concludes his childish escape from reality, the same yokels he previously conned during the Depression are now bailing him out once again, foreshadowing so many future bailouts of dishonest financiers whose assets should have been turned over to better management in bankruptcy court.

In one of the darkest moments of the film,

George Bailey's Christmas tree is jostled and one of the bells adorning it rings. George Bailey, now confident he and his fraudulent real estate scheme are safe, suggests the bell signifies an angel has earned his wings, as if his dishonest business dealings and ruthless defamation of legitimate competitors had divine sanction.

Nothing more is heard of Henry Potter, the man without to whom Bedford Falls owes its very existence. He is left friendless and without the one thing he could cling to before George Bailey, the Devil incarnate, tore it away: his honor. As the credits roll, evil has triumphed. The economic fallacies inherent in Baileyism become accepted truth, resulting in disaster after disaster, including the most recent in 2008.

CHAPTER 6

DICKENS' A CHRISTMAS CAROL HAS TOO

SAD AN ENDING FOR THE SEASON

No Christmas season would be complete

without stage or television productions of Charles

Dickens' unfortunately immortal *A Christmas Carol*.

The classic Reginald Owen and Alastair Sim movies

will no doubt play several times on multiple cable

channels. A few years back, we had a

live production shown at the Alleyway Theatre here in

Buffalo, N.Y. Or, you could always go full-on retro

and actually read the book.

I'm going to pass altogether this year on poor

Scrooge's story and hope for a sequel, even though

Dickens is no longer with us. It just doesn't get me

into the Christmas spirit to watch a story with such a

dark and foreboding ending. Christmas is supposed to

celebrate the birth of new hope.

As Butler Shaffer demonstrated in his

brilliant defense of poor Ebenezer, Scrooge was an

invaluable benefactor to English society before the

events of Dickens' story. We are not given details of

his business dealings other than they had something

to do with finance. That Scrooge had been in business

so many years and had amassed such wealth is

enough for us to conclude he had made many more

wise than unwise decisions on where to direct capital.

Who knows what housing, stores, factories,

railways or other benefits to society Scrooge had

made possible through his wise judgment? How many

thousands of jobs had he created? Dickens is unjustly

silent on this. Whatever Scrooge had financed, we

know it was something the public wanted or needed

enough to pay for voluntarily. Thanks to Scrooge,

however crusty his demeanor, the common people of

London were far richer than they otherwise would

have been without his services.

His only weakness seems to be sentimentality

towards the whiny, presumably mediocre Bob

Cratchett. We know Scrooge was paying Cratchett more than anyone else was willing to or Cratchett would surely have accepted a higher-paying job to put additional funds towards curing Tiny Tim. But we really don't have any evidence anyone else was willing to employ Cratchett at all, at any salary level. Still, we must defer to Scrooge's judgment on this and perhaps even laud him for finding a way to employ a substandard employee without jeopardizing the firm as a whole.

Thus, all was as well as it could have been on December 23. Scrooge's customers were happy, Bob Cratchett's was at least employed, thanks to Scrooge, and Scrooge himself was as happy as he could be, considering the ingratitude with which his genius had been rewarded and all the panhandlers constantly shaking him down.

Everything changed on Christmas Eve, when Scrooge was terrorized – there really is no other word for it – by three time-traveling, left wing apparitions. It wasn't enough to frighten an elderly man with the mere appearance of ghosts. They took him on a trip through time, scolding him for supposed mistakes made in the past and blaming him for the misfortunes of others in the present and future. And let's not forget the purpose of this psychological waterboarding. They are not, as Shaffer observes, pursuing Scrooge's happiness, but his money. They are William Graham Sumner's A & B conspiring to force C to relieve the suffering of X. Politicians A & B use the polite coercion of legislation; the spirits make use of more direct and honest threats of violence.

Their plot was successful. Scrooge awoke from his night of terror obviously out of his senses and began making one poor financial decision after another. Perhaps buying the largest turkey in the local shop could be excused on Christmas Day. But then, without any evidence of improvement in performance, he raised Bob Cratchett's salary and promised to take on the Cratchett family's medical expenses.

After that, we are told Scrooge was "transformed" completely, which we can only interpret to mean he no longer made the kind of decisions that had previously benefited so many. We are told Scrooge's subsequent behavior was so foolhardy that some people laughed at him. But even this wasn't enough to snap him out of the permanent delirium with which the spirits had inflicted him.

The story ends on that foreboding note. We are told Scrooge never again returned to the prudent decision-making that had brought on the supernatural terror attack on Christmas Eve. We have to assume the "transformed" Scrooge eventually went out of business, perhaps solely due to overpaying Cratchett, who is 50% of his labor force, perhaps due to the cumulative effect of the many unwise decisions we are told continued afterwards.

Not only was Tiny Tim's medical care cut off, but the whole Cratchett family was rendered destitute and starving. As Scrooge had already been paying Cratchett more than anyone else was willing to, even before the imprudent raise, we have to assume Cratchett made less after Scrooge went out of business than he did at the beginning of the story, if he convinced anyone to employ him at all.

Worse even than the misfortune that befell Scrooge, Cratchett and Tiny Tim was the misfortune visited upon society as a whole. How many profitable ventures were never financed, both before and after Scrooge went out of business from investing with his heart instead of his head? How many future jobs were destroyed and children of unemployed fathers left sick and hungry?

Certainly, this horror story would be better told on Halloween than Christmas. Christmas is a hopeful holiday, celebrating the birth of the savior of the world, whose parable of the three servants lauds wise capital investment and condemns unwise use of capital. We can only hope some ambitious writer will pen a sequel to Dickens' dark tale, in which Scrooge regains his senses, fires Bob Cratchett and returns to making the kind of decisions that once raised the

living standards of so many.

CHAPTER 7

AN ANTI-STATE CHRISTMAS

Well, here we are, about to celebrate our second
Christmas in the "new normal." No doubt many are
wondering if they can still catch the last train to
Sombertown, where at least they're sure they'll be
allowed to earn a living. As bad as Burgermeister

Meisterburger was, he never outlawed that. Neither did he ban Christmas altogether, as Anthony Fauci would like to do. As of this writing, Fauci had just told CBS News it was "too soon to tell" if Christmas gatherings would be permissible.

Ironically, the state attempts to cast compliance with its authoritarian edicts as "selflessness." We must sacrifice those things that make life worth living, they tell us, for the good of everyone else. Exercising the inalienable rights to life, liberty, and the pursuit of happiness - or even just wishing to return to the overregulated lives we led in 2019 - is "selfish."

Everyone who believes in freedom is eventually accused of selfishness. Libertarians often make it easier for the statists to sell this canard by declaring inviolate "my rights," or "my liberty." There isn't anything wrong with that, but the non-aggression principle really isn't primarily about oneself. It's about what one can and cannot do to other people.

The American principles of natural rights and liberty, derived from John Locke's Second Treatise of Government, contain the proposition that no power can be delegated to a government that people do not possess as individuals in the state of nature – the state without government. Does anyone really believe any individual has an inherent right to lock other people in their homes unless and until they prove they have received a vaccine or tested negative for a virus? Of course not. It's absurd on its face.

Everyone has a right to take whatever precautions they believe necessary to protect their own health, as long as they do not invade the rights of others. That means staying at home if one believes leaving home is too risky. But no one has a right to force others to stay in their homes, take a vaccine, or wear a mask, even if those measures were effective. This is true selfishness – invading the rights of others for one's own benefit.

Neither does anyone have the right to force someone else to subsidize their decision to stay home. How can one person be forced to work, assuming all the risks of working, to earn the money needed to pay someone else to stay home and avoid those same risks? Are we not all created equal?

What Would Jesus Do?

There is nothing Christian about the new totalitarianism, either. Certainly, "do unto others as you would have them do unto you" cannot include forcing anyone to be injected with a drug or denying them the right to feed their families. Nowhere in the gospels does Jesus force anyone to do anything. The entire thrust of his message is that salvation must be chosen voluntarily. He'd certainly never advocate empowering the hypocritical Pharisees whom he spends all of his ministry ridiculing or the brutal Roman state to force people to follow his commandments.

Some people imagine Jesus would want us to suffer in silence under government oppression, offering no resistance to authorities, as if merely absorbing punishment could buy us salvation. They ought to pick up a New Testament and read it some time, because the Jesus found there does no such thing. Yes, he insists on non-violence, except when dealing with banksters. But nowhere does he set an example of silent compliance with government corruption or tyranny.

Certainly, the Jesus who faced down and defied Pontius Pilate, the most powerful man in the Judea of his time, would never be intimidated by a sniveling little bureaucrat like Fauci. Jesus would see right through him, treating him to a healthy dose of the same withering invective he loosed upon the Pharisees. Then, he'd ignore government edicts that do nothing but harm just as he ignored the Pharisees who tried to keep him from healing the man with the withered hand on the sabbath.

Let's not forget that Fauci really doesn't exercise any power over us. He merely issues recommendations. It wasn't even the federal government that closed businesses or issued mask mandates for most of the pandemic. Those decisions were made by state governors exercising powers granted them in the various "state of emergency" legislation in the various states.

So, it is much more important to know where your

state government stands than to listen to anything Fauci says. If you're in Iowa, Florida, Texas, or any other of the "free states" as far as Covid restrictions are concerned, this Christmas may not be substantively different than those before 2020. And even if you're in a lockdown state like New York or California, find out where your county sheriff or municipal police chief stands. If they've made statements indicating they aren't going to enforce capacity limits on family gatherings or private events, the predatory state has no teeth.

But What Can I Do?

Standing up to tyranny is never easy. With the media relentlessly disseminating the government's propaganda, it can seem like you're completely alone in your dissent. You're not. Let me tell you a story from before this current nightmare began.

Most of us remember that before we were instructed to be terrified of Covid-19, it was terrorists. And just like we are presently asked to accept as "gospel" that lockdowns, mask mandates, and the new vaccines are effective against the spread of the virus, we were then expected to believe the DC Empire's overseas wars were effective in preventing terrorism. "Support the troops" meant supporting the wars despite the clear evidence it was those very wars and the military and covert operations that preceded them that motivated terrorist attacks in the first place.

The effect of the propaganda campaign was what can only be described as a cultish veneration for the military by the private sector. People fell over themselves to thank anyone in a government costume for his service, not knowing if this person had ever been anywhere near a live battlefield. This isn't to say the average private or specialist deserves the blame for decisions made orders of magnitude above his rank or pay grade to go to war. But if the wars were not benefiting the people who paid for them – but rather making the problem worse - why is gratitude appropriate?

It was during this war fever that I found myself at the gate for a late flight home after a long business trip. There is always the anxiety when taking a flight late in the day that there will be some problem and, instead of spending the evening with your family, you might find yourself in an airport hotel for the night. But as luck would have it, this flight began to board. That's when I heard the announcement that is likely familiar to everyone.

"First class passengers and military personnel in uniform are welcome to board at this time."

Don't ask me why I chose that moment to say it. I had been traveling for business for almost two decades at that point and it had run through my mind every time I heard this particular announcement since the "War on Terror" began. But that late afternoon, waiting at the gate with that film that seems to cover you after a day of meetings and rushing to the airport, it just came out.

"I'm in a taxpayer uniform. Can I get on the plane now, too?"

You can imagine what happened next, but it didn't. Having desecrated one of the great civic pieties of the time, I was not scolded by the airline employee nor assaulted by any of the passengers waiting to board (one of which turned out to be active-duty military who thanked me for saying it). Instead, just like the Grinch who did hear a sound rising over the snow that started in low and then started to grow, I heard….laughter.

It wasn't uproarious laughter. It was laughter that started out nervous and very gradually became more comfortable. And it was an absolute epiphany for me. I discovered I wasn't alone in what I thought before uttering the blasphemy. Everyone laughing was thinking it, too, but were just too afraid to say it. They were afraid of what others might think, or what might happen to them if they spoke up, or just afraid to say something they were told they weren't allowed to say. I've never forgotten that moment.

Questioning the state's official dogma regarding the military in 2011 is no different than questioning the Covid regime in 2021. Those people nervously laughing at the airport gate are all around you right now. Even if they haven't read the numerous randomized controlled trial studies indicating lockdowns, mask mandates, and other non-pharmaceutical interventions (NPIs) don't have any effect on the virus or that natural immunity is as good or better than vaccine-induced immunity, their common sense is telling them something is dreadfully wrong.

They want to speak up but are too afraid to do so. But they'll rally to you if you have the courage they lack.

Speaking up does not come without cost. There is a chance it may cause friction with family or friends. It's especially difficult because we're often faced with the situation in which people we like and care about can reflexively repeat demonstrably false regime talking points they heard on major media outlets without any negative consequences at parties or other social gatherings. But the moment you respond with anything even questioning the official narrative, you're not only viewed as a kook by your own kith and kin but admonished for "bringing up politics."

You may also find that your ability to disseminate information on the largest social media platforms becomes curtailed, not only by the platforms themselves banning or "shadow banning" you, but your own friends and family "unfriending" or blocking you. Such is the price of telling the treasonous truth in an "empire of lies," as Orwell would put it.

Every individual has to decide if and when to speak up. It all comes down to what the Austrian economists would call your "value scale." Do you value your relationship with those family members and friends who may disassociate with you and/or your standing on social media platforms more or less than telling the truth and striking a blow for freedom? It comes down to that.

In making that decision, I'd advise avoiding the excuse that "one person/voice can't make a difference." That's a false dichotomy. The radical left and the MAGA right are both comprised of individuals. While no single one of them could change much, the individual decisions of those who comprise those groups is what makes those groups movements. Neither one represents a majority of Americans, but they have both influenced the direction of American politics substantially.

When to speak up may at first seem like a more difficult question. If we're saying just celebrating Christmas like we did in 2019 is a revolutionary act, do we really need to muck it up with possible friction over political issues? Again, it all comes down to your value scale. How many times of year do you see as many people as you do during the holidays? When are they more likely to take what you have to say to heart — while having a drink face to face or on a social media thread? Is freedom worth risking a little friction at a time when the federal and state governments are musing out loud about whether to let you celebrate at all?

The statists hate freedom, and they never take a Christmas vacation. Holiday propaganda like "A Christmas Carol" and "It's a Wonderful Life" were written by avowed socialists for the express purpose of representing economic freedom as ugly and selfish. These are humorless, joyless people whose only gratification seems to be wagging their fingers at anyone who doesn't share their resentment at the idea that someone, somewhere, might be having a good time.

Freedom and civil society are under assault by a

cabal whose power over resources and information is unrivaled by any empire in history. Academia and the media resent that the market rewards the innovation and hard work of entrepreneurs more than it rewards them, or even that people not as wealthy as they can live happy, independent lives without subscribing to their "progressive" religion. "Why, some of these people have dirty fingernails and old-fashioned beliefs!" they lament. The super-rich, even those who made their money honestly in the marketplace, believe their success proves they are wise enough to make choices for everyone.

Together, this unholy alliance seeks the power of the state to force the rest of society to conform to its wishes. And don't be fooled. It's not public safety or fairness they're after. It's obedience. That's why hard evidence their policies haven't worked is useless. They aren't interested in results; they're interested in compliance. Never mind that without a free society their way of life will cease to exist.

What better time to emulate the great libertarian from Galilee, who never once attempted to use the power of the Jewish or Roman states to enforce his commandments. "Love one another, as I have loved you," he said, and did so even when the state made it illegal (Mark 3: 1-6). Neither was he afraid of who he might offend by telling the truth. Now, more than ever, we need the courage to follow his example. It may be difficult, but I doubt any of us will end up nailed to a piece of wood. At least not literally.

Let's not forget Jesus' story ended happily and so can ours. Freedom can rise from the dead. All it will take is a little Christlike courage to hold the hypocrites of our own time in contempt and tell the Pontius

Pilates who threaten us with the power of the state to go pound sand. As Senator Rand Paul recently reminded us, they can't arrest us all.

What better time than Christmas to bring back joy and freedom to the world?

Let's Get in the Mood

I hope you've enjoyed this little book and had a few laughs along the way. Whether you're religious or not, the Christmas season reminds us of all the best things about humanity: peace on earth, goodwill towards men, universal brotherhood, and the opportunity for a new life. These are the things Thomas Paine was thinking about when he wrote, "Society is in every state a blessing."

He also said government "in its best state is but a necessary evil; in its worst state an intolerable one."

Some of us think he was absolutely right – except for the "necessary" part.

In any case, there has never been a more appropriate year for an anti-state Christmas. It's the birthday of a man murdered by the government for threatening its power with a simple message of love and respect for one's neighbor. The least we can do in return is ignore the government's ridiculous edicts and restore the perennial tradition of returning to the true foundations of civil society: family, friends, and faith.

It never hurts to start with a celebratory beverage. One of my favorite Christmas memories is being in Hamburg, Germany on business in December and visiting a traditional German Christmas market. My German hosts and I enjoyed shopping for gifts, munching on roasted chestnuts, and listening to the music as we roamed from shop to shop. But the highlight of the evening was definitely standing around an outdoor barrel fire and drinking Gluhwein ("glow wine"). One cup of this Yuletide nectar and you're guaranteed to feel warm in any climate – even here in the wilds of Western New York.

Of course, I wanted to share the experience with my American friends and family, so, when I returned home, I began searching for recipes on the internet. I tried several in an attempt to duplicate what I had been served in Hamburg. After some modifications, I came up with the following. Try it outdoors, around a campfire, singing Christmas carols or talking a little treason.

Ingredients:

1   orange

1   lemon

20   whole cloves

3   cinnamon sticks

1   gallon Burgundy wine

1   cup sugar

Optional: 12-14 ounces vodka or rum (about ½ of a 750 ml bottle)

Directions:

1.   Cut the orange and the lemon in halves. Poke 5 cloves into the rinds of each.

2.   Add orange and lemon halves with cloves, wine, and cinnamon sticks to a large pot and bring to boil.

3.   Lower heat and simmer covered for about 45 minutes.

4.   Remove cloves from orange and lemon and squeeze juice from both back into pot.

5. Stir in sugar

6. Add vodka or rum and stir. Or, add a shot of vodka or rum to each glass instead of adding 12-14 ounces to the whole batch.

7. Serve hot.

Hint: In mid-2000s Hamburg, they made it without vodka or rum, but offered an added shot of vodka per cup as an option. Either way, please do not plan on driving after enjoying this beverage – it will sneak up on you!

Once back inside, there is nothing better than getting everyone together in your living room or family room, in front of a fireplace if you have one, for another great Christmas tradition. I've made a few modifications to this seasonal favorite that you can read aloud to your attendees:

The Night Before (New Normal) Christmas

'Twas the night before Christmas, when all through the town

Not a creature was stirring, all were safely locked down;

The masks were all hung by the chimney with care

In hopes that St. Fauci soon would be there;

The children were nestled all snug in their beds,

While visions of booster shots invaded their heads;

And mamma in her kerchief, and I in my cap,

Lay six feet apart for a long winter's nap,

When out on the lawn there arose such a clatter,

I sprang from the bed to see what was the matter.

Away to the window I flew like a flash,

Tore open the shutters and threw up the sash.

The moon on the breast of the new-fallen snow

Gave the lustre of mid-day to objects below,

When, what did my wondering eyes see arrive,

But a government agent, walking straight up my drive,

As bureaucrats go, he was lively and quick,

And I despaired in a moment of avoiding the prick.

More rapid than eagles had the variants come,

And he whistled, and shouted, and called one by one:

"Now, Alpha! now, Beta! now, Gamma and Delta!

On, Eta! on, Epsilon! Kappa and Lambda!

I have the new shot; there's no reason to stall.

I've got the jab that will dash away all!"

He was dressed very badly, from his head to his toe,

It was hard to imagine a girl dating this schmo;

A bundle of needles he had flung on his back,

And he looked like a peddler just opening his pack.

He was chubby and plump, from his tax-derived pelf,

And I cringed when I saw him, in spite of myself;

The dim look in his eye and small size of his head,

Soon gave me to know I had plenty to dread;

He spoke not a word, but tried straight away,

To stab all our arms with the new mRNA,

But laying a finger on each side of his nose,

I gave it a squeeze and got him up on his toes;

He sprang to his car as my boot hit his rear,

And away did he drive almost too fast to steer.

To the neighbors I shouted, ere he drove out of

sight,

"Happy Christmas to all, and to all a good-night."

Merry Christmas to you and yours, and a Happy, Freer, New Year.

An Anti-State Christmas

ABOUT THE AUTHOR

Tom Mullen hosts the *Tom Mullen Talks Freedom* podcast and is the author of *Where Do Conservatives and Liberals Come From? And What Ever Happened to Life, Liberty, and the Pursuit of Happiness?* and *A Return to Common Sense: Reawakening Liberty in the Inhabitants of America.* His writing has been featured in Newsweek, The Huffington Post, The Washington Times, RealClear Markets, LewRockwell.com, and The Foundation for Economic Education. His podcast episodes and writing can be found at www.tommullentalksfreedom.com.

Tom is originally a native of Buffalo, NY and a graduate of Canisius College. He earned a master's degree in English from State University of New York College at Buffalo. He now resides with his family in Western New York.

Made in the USA
Monee, IL
27 November 2021

83112129R00059